WORLD'S GREATEST MOUNTAINS

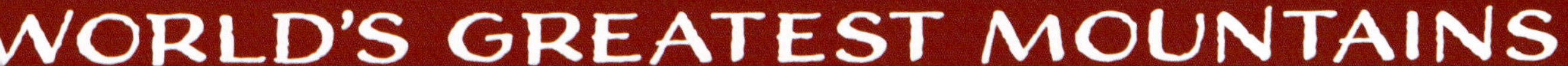

Exploring K2

Kashmir's Savage Mountain

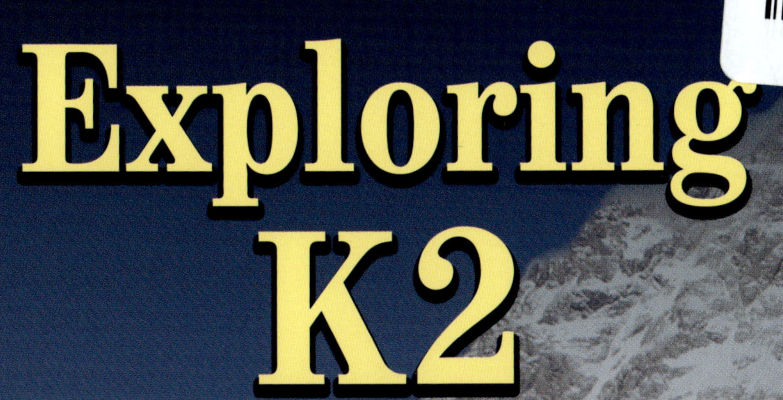

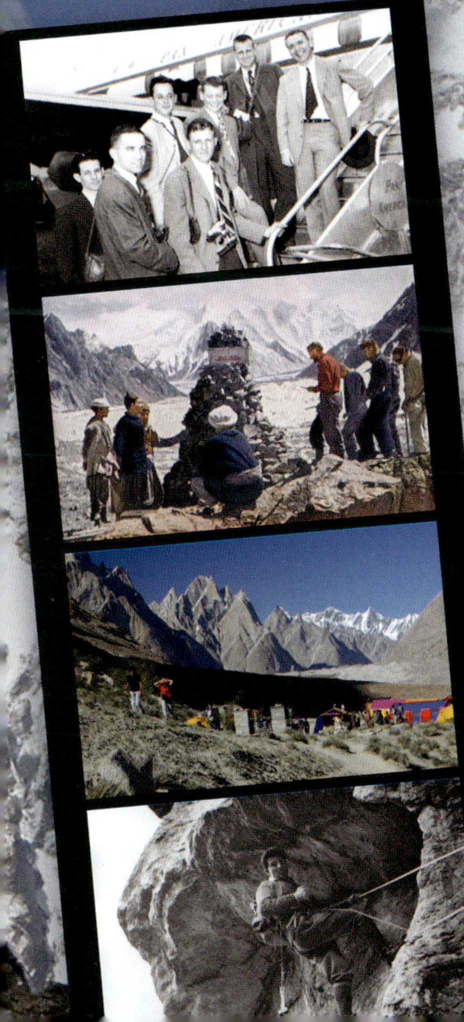

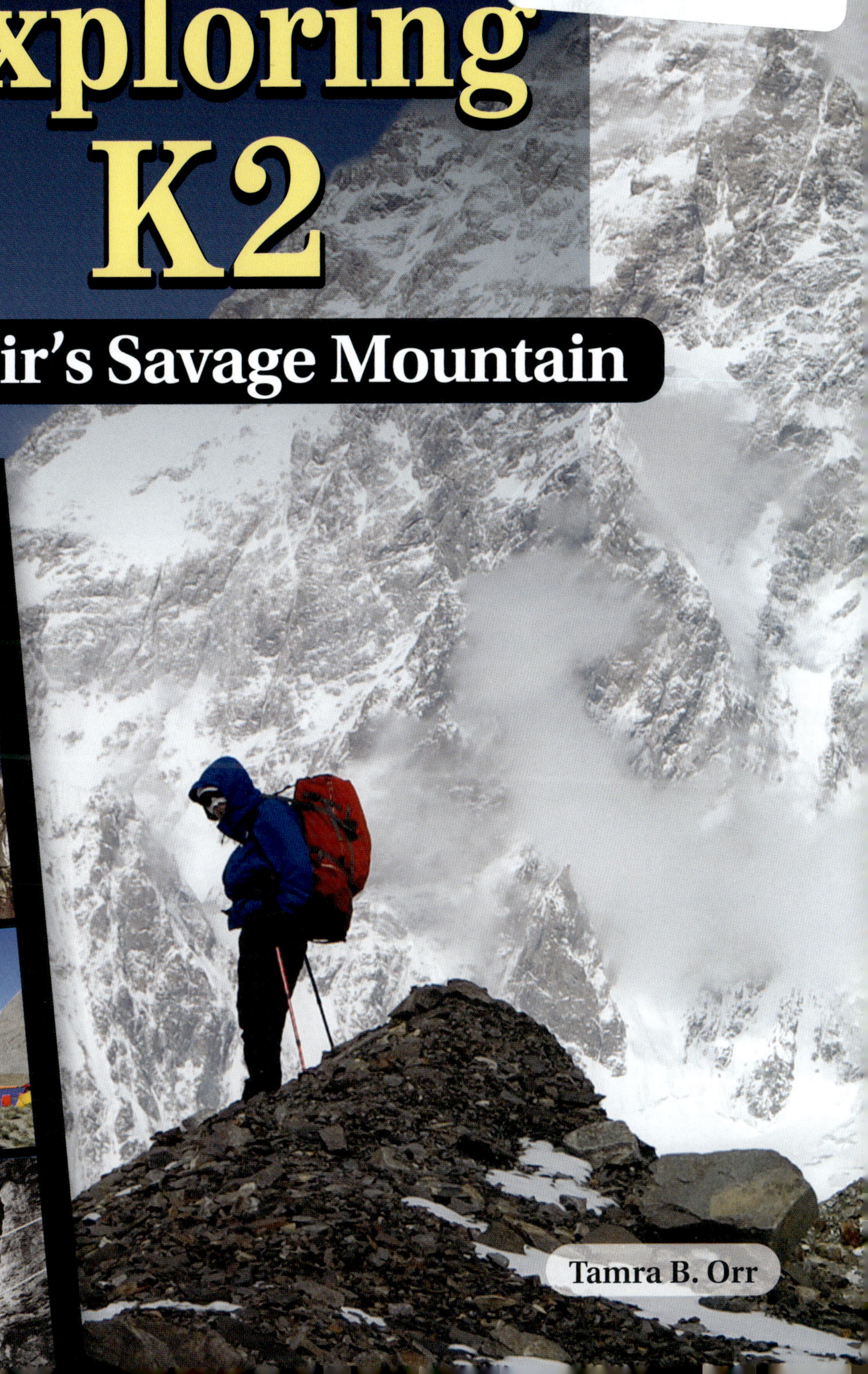

Tamra B. Orr

© 2024 by Curious Fox Books™, an imprint of Fox Chapel Publishing Company, Inc.

Exploring K2 is a revision, first published in 2014 by Purple Toad Publishing, Inc. Reproduction of its contents is strictly prohibited without written permission from the rights holder.

Paperback ISBN 979-8-8909-4117-6
Hardcover ISBN 979-8-8909-4118-3

The Cataloging-in-Publication Data is on file with the Library of Congress.

To learn more about the other great books from Fox Chapel Publishing, or to find a retailer near you, call toll-free 800-457-9112, send mail to 903 Square Street, Mount Joy, PA 17552, or visit us at *www.FoxChapelPublishing.com*.

We are always looking for talented authors. To submit an idea, please send a brief inquiry to acquisitions@foxchapelpublishing.com.

Fox Chapel Publishing makes every effort to use environmentally friendly paper for printing.

Printed in Malaysia

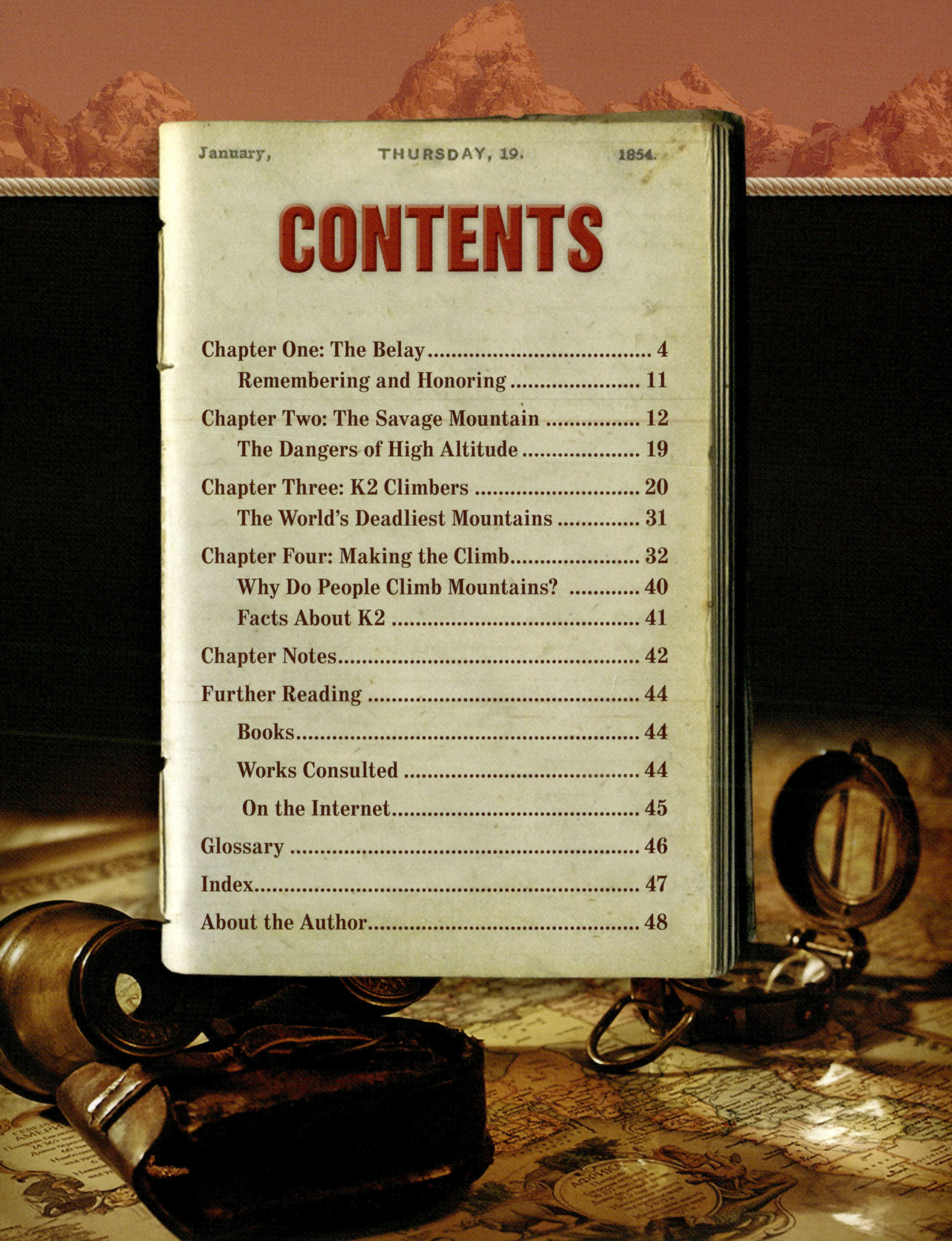

CONTENTS

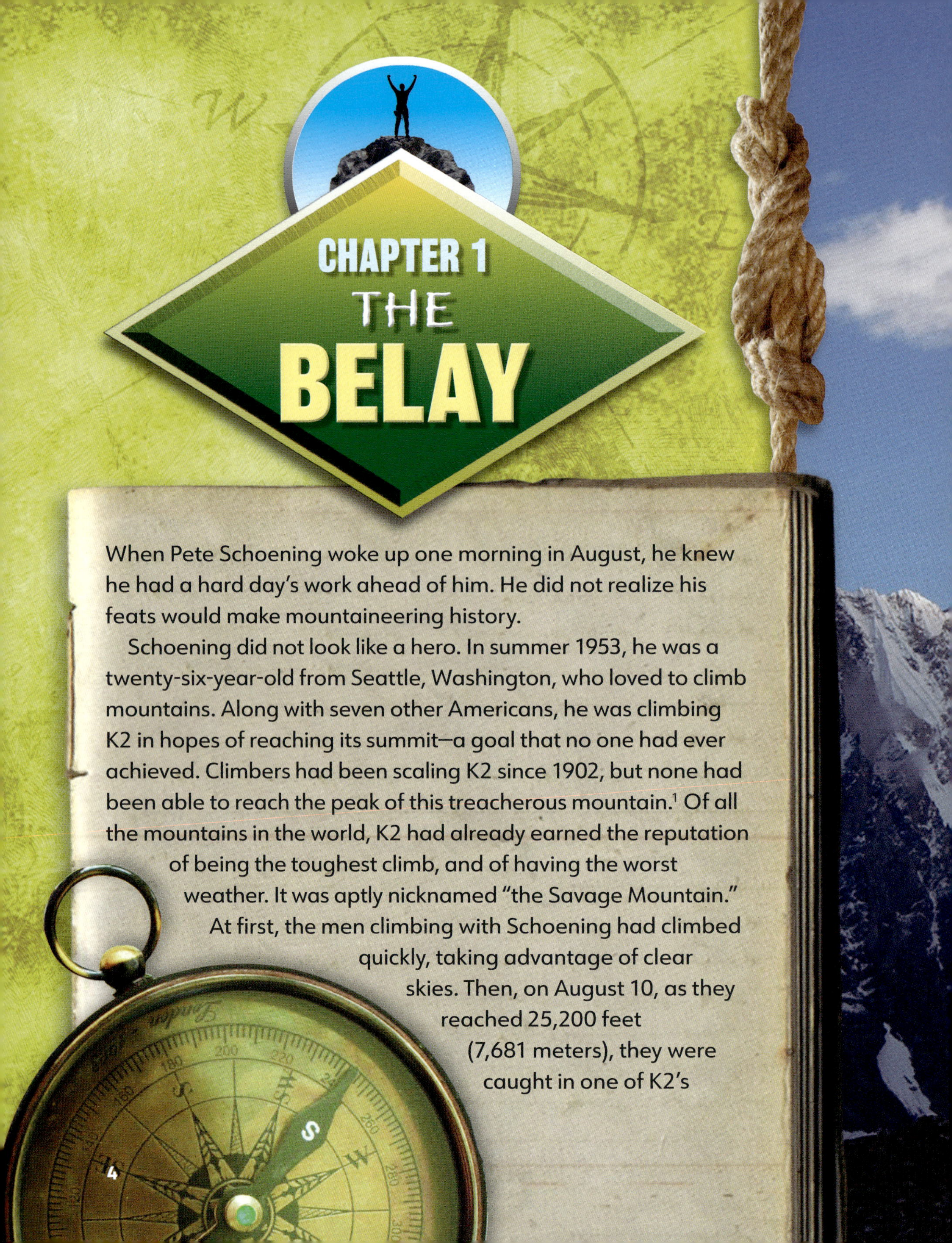

When Pete Schoening woke up one morning in August, he knew he had a hard day's work ahead of him. He did not realize his feats would make mountaineering history.

Schoening did not look like a hero. In summer 1953, he was a twenty-six-year-old from Seattle, Washington, who loved to climb mountains. Along with seven other Americans, he was climbing K2 in hopes of reaching its summit—a goal that no one had ever achieved. Climbers had been scaling K2 since 1902, but none had been able to reach the peak of this treacherous mountain.[1] Of all the mountains in the world, K2 had already earned the reputation of being the toughest climb, and of having the worst weather. It was aptly nicknamed "the Savage Mountain." At first, the men climbing with Schoening had climbed quickly, taking advantage of clear skies. Then, on August 10, as they reached 25,200 feet (7,681 meters), they were caught in one of K2's

K2's beauty and majesty draw climbers from all over the world, but hidden beneath the mountain's splendor is incredible danger.

The seven men who climbed aboard the plane in 1953 had no idea of the challenge waiting ahead on K2. From left to right, on tarmac: Bill White (expedition agent), Art Gilkey, and Bob Craig; on stairs: George Bell, Pete Schoening, Dee Molenaar, and Charles Houston. (Robert Bates and Tony Streather were awaiting the team in Pakistan.)

unpredictable blizzards. The men huddled inside their tents for ten days, trying to wait out the storm, stay warm, and not use up their food supplies.

Disaster

A bad situation turned much worse when climber Art Gilkey developed a blood clot in his leg.[2] Though never verified, it is suspected the clot then moved to his lungs, resulting in a pulmonary embolism that restricted his blood flow. It became it impossible for him to walk—or climb. The men knew they had no choice. They had to get Gilkey back down to base camp, which was 9,000 feet (2,743 meters) below. It was his only chance for survival.

Going down K2 is more difficult than going up it. Going down in a blizzard with an injured man would be nearly impossible. Every climber on the team knew this, but they felt they had no choice. They were in this together, and if one man was in trouble, it was up to the rest to rescue him. Charles Houston and Robert Bates, who had been part of the team, recounted in their book *K2: The Savage Mountain* that the bonds between the men had become so strong that none of them even thought of leaving Gilkey and saving themselves. As they prepared to descend, according to Houston, "Little was spoken. Each of us realized that he was beginning the most dangerous day's work of his lifetime."[4]

The next few hours were worse than the climbers could have imagined. The men struggled to move Gilkey down the slippery mountain. Wrapped in a sleeping bag and tent and lashed to a makeshift stretcher, Gilkey did his best to shout encouragement to his teammates. He knew what impossible odds they were all facing.

The men wore every piece of clothing they had brought, but they were still crippled by the bitter cold. Icicles clung to their beards, mustaches, and eyebrows as they worked to belay Gilkey, lowering him by rope, over sharp ledges and icy slopes. At one point, their ropes caused a mini-avalanche, covering the men in snow before it thundered by.[5]

A Hero's Moment

For hours, the men worked to get Gilkey down the mountain. Their fingers were so numb inside their gloves that it was becoming increasingly difficult to handle equipment. Their feet had lost almost all

Pete Schoening

feeling. Their snow goggles kept icing over, so they had to lift them to see clearly.

Finally, the men were faced with a slope of ice too hard for their axes to chip, and at such a steep angle, there was no way to climb down it. Their plan was to swing Gilkey's stretcher across to a safe ledge where everyone could rest for a moment.

Suddenly, climber George Bell lost his footing. He began to slide. As he careened down the ice, his rope tangled with the ropes of his teammates. Like a doomed row of dominoes, each man was pulled down, one by one, over the edge. They flung out their arms, trying to grab something with their axes, but not one was able to do so.

Five men began plummeting toward the Earth. Years later, Houston and Bates wrote, "Only thousands of feet of empty space separated us from the glacier below. It was like falling off a slanting Empire State Building six times as high as the real one."[6]

The weight of his entire team pulled on the rope wound around Pete Schoening's waist.[7] The only thing keeping him from following the rest of them over the side was the ice axe he had dug into the snow earlier. Now he clutched it with both hands, putting the weight on the head of the axe and hoping it would hold.

It did—as did Schoening's grip. Slowly, the men below began climbing back up their ropes to solid

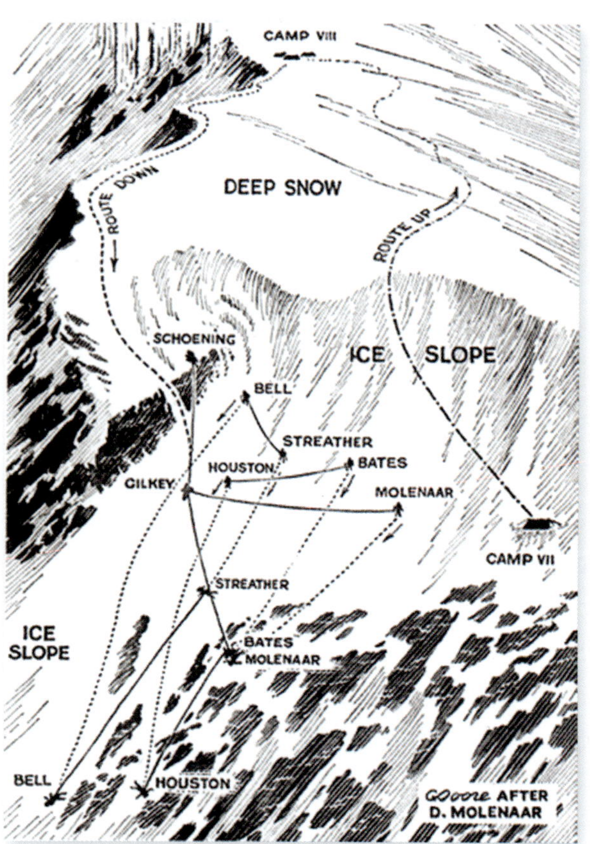

A 1953 drawing shows where each man was positioned when disaster struck.

land. Several were injured, but all were alive.

Schoening was humble about what he had done, praising luck more than anything else. Later, Bates wrote, ". . . one man had held five men who slid 150 to 300 feet down a 45-degree slope and that he had done it at nearly 25,000 feet, where the mere job of survival absorbs most of the strength of a man. Such magnificent belay work has rarely been recorded in mountaineering anywhere."[8] Today, the moment is still referred to as "The Belay."

An Unexpected Disappearance

Knowing they would not last if they didn't take time to rest, eat, and check their injuries, the men began putting up a tent. For a few moments, they concentrated on battling the high winds and piercing cold to get the tent anchored. It took enormous effort. As Bates and Houston wrote, "It was like working in the slipstream behind an airplane as it taxied across the snow, spraying stinging particles behind."[9]

At last, it was time to pull Gilkey off the icy slope where he had been waiting for so long. When two teammates went to get him, however, they were shocked to discover the stretcher, and the axes holding it in place, were gone! Somehow, as the men had worked frantically to erect the tent, Gilkey had been swept off the ice to his death thousands of feet below. Perhaps another small avalanche had passed through where he was, or perhaps the axes had lost their grip. His remains would not be found for another forty years, but the mystery of how he fell would never be solved.

His teammates were in shock. Their night was spent in grief—and pain. One man had a deep gash on his leg and cracked ribs. Another had a concussion. All of the men had varying degrees of frostbite. It was a long night—with an even longer descent in store for them the next day.

Eventually, the men made it back to base camp. A few days later, they were home. Schoening went on to get married, have six children, and create a very successful manufacturing business. Before passing away in 2004 from cancer, he had scaled five of the seven highest mountains in the world. Fellow climber Nick Clinch describes his friend: "He had the strength of a bull and heart of a Boy Scout. His physical strength, leadership, and personality were central to his expeditions."[10] Teammate Dee Molenaar, who had been part of the 1953 K2 disaster, recalled his friend when he told *The Seattle Times,* "He was a prince of a human being. . . . [without him,] I'm sure we would have all gone down."[11]

Once again, the summit of K2 was missed. The wicked mountain, known worldwide for its difficulty and high death toll, had beaten yet another expedition. The fight was not over, however. On July 31, 1954, Achille Compagnoni and Lino Lacedelli reached the summit as part of an Italian expedition led by Ardito Desio. It would take Americans another 24 years to do the same. with climber Jim Wickwire reaching the summit via a new route on September 6, 1978. Even today, the battle to beat the mountain continues as climbers shoulder their packs, strap on boots, and head up into the clouds in search of conquest.

The team builds a memorial to Art Gilkey on K2 in 1953.

To honor the memory of Art Gilkey, as well as other climbers who have died on K2, a memorial was created in 1953 at the mountain's base camp. It is made of gray rocks and boulders. Silver tins with the names and dates of climbers engraved on them sparkle in the sunshine. Various trinkets and pieces of climbing equipment are stuck between the rocks. Climbers often take a moment to stop by the memorial and remember those who lost their lives in the attempt to conquer the mountain.[12]

In 2006, Karen Molenaar Terrell, daughter of Dee Molenaar, brought together the children and grandchildren of the men who had been on the famous K2 expedition more than 50 years earlier. Calling themselves "The Children of the Belay," they numbered more than thirty and represented three generations. They gathered that year to celebrate the fact that, without Schoening's heroics, none of them would have existed.[13]

Schoening's axe that saved his life and the lives of his team now hangs in the Bradford Washburn American Mountaineering Museum in Golden, Colorado.[14]

The memorial to Art Gilkey gives climbers a chance to appreciate the sacrifices that have come before them, and the inspiration to be extra careful when making the journey themselves.

Grab an atlas or go on the internet and look at all the mountain ranges crisscrossing the planet. Some are covered in pine trees, while others are carpeted in rich soils of brown velvet. Some mountains are blanketed in green grasses, and others are draped with countless acres of snow.

If you are looking for the tallest mountains in the world, spin the globe until you find the northern regions of Asia, near Pakistan and India. Here the Himalayas, Karakoram, Hindu Kush, and Hindu Raj all form one of the world's most incredible mountain ranges. The region boasts hundreds of mountains that soar 20,000 feet (6,100 meters) or more up into the sky. There are 60 peaks touching 23,000 feet (7,010 meters), and five that top out at 26,000 feet (7,925 meters). Two of these—Mount Everest and K2—have been attracting mountain climbers for over a century and a half.[1]

The Karakoram range is about 300 miles (500 kilometers) long and is the home of huge mountains

Some parts of K2 are fairly straightforward to climb, while others feature sharp edges, walls of ice, and treacherous ground.

This region is lined by the most imposing mountains in the world.

and hundreds of creeping glaciers.[2] This is also where you will find K2, often referred to as the Savage Mountain. It has earned its nickname! K2 got its simple name in 1852, when a British surveyor named T. G. Montgomerie was cataloging as many of the distant peaks as he could. He chose the name K2 because it was the second peak surveyed in the Karakoram, the range in which this giant stands.[3]

Remote and Empty

Unlike many other mountain regions, there are no people who live on or even close to K2. Most villages are weeks away from the base of the mountain. For climbers in trouble, rescue by helicopter is the only option—and then only at base camps, and only if the weather is not too foggy, windy, or snowy for pilots to navigate.

The people who live in the shadow of the Karakoram mountain range are a mix of cultures from Afghanistan, Central Asia, China, and India.[4] The majority of them are Muslim and farm for a living. Many grow wheat, barley, and apricots, which thrive on the valley floors. The people depend on irrigation since there is little rainfall in the area. Many people in the villages spend their days making sure the canals for channeling water from melting snow and glaciers are in good working order.

Finding K2 is more than a little challenging. It is so remote that it cannot be easily seen from any town or village. The closest town is Askole on the Pakistan side, and it is over 65 miles (105 kilometers) away. This small village is referred to as the "gateway to high mountains and glaciers."[5] Here is where expedition leaders hire porters to help carry their gear, equipment, and food to base camp. The journey takes from six to eight days by foot. Porters are often heavily weighed down, although some bring along ponies to carry extra cargo. Traveling to the mountain's base camp is one of the most expensive and time-consuming

Most of the people crossing this bridge into the town of Askole are either locals or climbers in search of adventure.

Base camp at K2.

parts of the journey for climbers.

In addition to being isolated, there are other reasons for K2's nickname. Because it is the tallest of the mountains around it, it gets some of the harshest weather. Predicting what the weather will be like is almost impossible, as it can be sunny and calm on one side and fiercely cold and windy on the other. K2 is known to have winds up to 140 miles per hour (225 kilometers per hour), unexpected fog, monsoon rains at lower elevations, and terrible blizzards and frequent avalanches higher up. Climbers only attempt to reach the top of the mountain during the summer months (June, July, and August) because these have the safest weather. Even during these months, temperatures near the top can drop to between −40°F and −50°F (−40°C and −46°C), and storms can come from seemingly nowhere.

Along with these challenges, recent global warming changes have affected the climate of the mountain. Shrinking glaciers bring an increased risk of rock falls, avalanches, and the collapse of seracs or overhangs of ice. It also makes it harder to secure equipment because the snow is softer, and the ice is less reliable as a source of stability.[6] In addition to its height and weather patterns, K2 also has many sharp cliff edges and entire slopes of ice at 45-degree angles.

Up to 7,000 feet (2,133 meters), walnut, elm, willow, and poplar trees grow, watered by the snowmelt in spring. Although firs, pine, and spruce grow as high as 10,500 feet (3,200 meters), by 12,000 feet (3,657 meters), the only living plants are dwarf willows. Here and there, near valley streams, meadows of honeysuckle and rhododendrons are found.[7] But above 12,000 feet (3,657 meters), there are virtually no plants or animals because the weather is too harsh for anything to survive. The land is made up of little more than snow, ice, and stone.

In the lower levels of these mountain ranges, a few fascinating creatures roam. Snow leopards wander through in search of Tibetan sheep and other tasty prey. The leopard's thick fur and wide feet help it keep warm and avoid slipping on rocks. Using its tail to stay balanced, a snow leopard can leap as far as 50 feet (15 meters) in one bound. These animals are endangered, and experts believe there are only a few thousand left roaming through the Himalayas.[8] Other animals in the lower elevations include the wild yak with its long, shaggy coat, and the Tibetan antelope, a runner that can reach speeds of up to 50 miles per hour (80 kilometers per hour).[9]

Tibetan antelopes

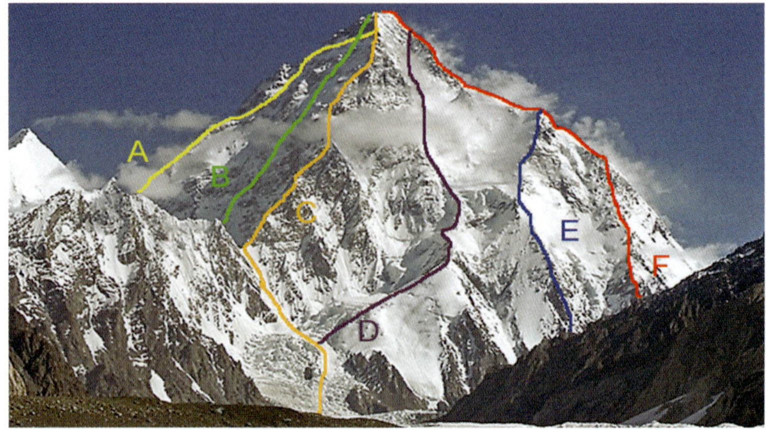

These are the southern routes that have been climbed on K2: A: West Ridge; B: West Face; C: Southwest Pillar; D: South Face; E: South-southeast Spur; F: Abruzzi Spur.

The Shape of the Mountain

Millions of years ago, the tectonic plates under India and Asia collided, creating some of the world's biggest mountains.[10] The huge Karakoram Mountains began forming about 40 million years ago. They were molded by a series of ice ages over the last million years, as well as by thousands of years of erosion. Even with all these changes, the height of K2 has not changed greatly in the last few hundred years. Its prominence is a staggering 28,251 feet (8,611 meters).

K2 is made up of four different ridges. These are the Abruzzi Spur on the southeast side, Negrotto Pass and Angel Peak on the southwest side, Junction Peak on the northeast, and Savoia Pass on the northwest.[11] Over the years, climbers have come up with ten different routes up these ridges. Some have been quite successful. The Abruzzi Spur is the most popular. Other routes were attempted once, but never again.

K2 is a dangerous mountain. Even the walk from the Askole to the base camp is so difficult that only seasoned trekkers are able to do it. It is frozen and isolated—and yet, for some, it is an invitation to survive a challenge. Whether the mountain or its climbers will win is always the question—and it's one that people keep asking.

The Dangers of High Altitude

The human body can adapt to being thousands of feet in the air or far underwater. It can cope with triple-digit high temperatures and subzero low temperatures. This ability to adapt is known as "acclimatizing."

While the body can adapt to these extremes, there is often a price. Mountain climbers know this rule quite well. Climbing the world's tallest peaks puts a huge strain on the body and increases the risk of a number of health problems.

When going to high elevations, the body has to shift how it operates. Breathing and heart rate speed up to deliver more oxygen to cells. Blood flow to the brain increases, and the body even develops more capillaries to increase efficiency. People who have trouble acclimatizing develop "altitude sickness." This condition is caused by a lack of oxygen in the body. Climbing too fast, spending too much time in extreme altitudes, and lack of rest and water will increase a person's risk for altitude sickness.

There are several stages of altitude sickness. Acute mountain sickness typically occurs at altitudes above 8,000 feet (2,438 meters). Symptoms include headache, nausea, and edema. With edema, your body cannot get rid of fluid properly, and your hands and feet will swell. High altitude pulmonary edema (HAPE) affects the lungs, and high altitude cerebral edema (HACE) affects the brain. Each of these stages is serious. When symptoms begin, the only real treatment is to get to lower elevations as quickly as possible.[12]

Headaches are often an early sign of altitude sickness.

Most people look at photographs and films of the world's highest mountains and marvel at nature's beauty from the comfort of their living rooms. They may not even notice the blinding white snow, the sharp black mountain ridges, and the incredible heights.

A number of outdoor fans choose to head out to appreciate the snow and slopes up close through the sports of skiing, snowboarding, or snowmobiling. Tourists also travel to exotic locations and appreciate views of soaring mountain ranges from cozy hotels, cruise ships, or winter resorts.

And then there are those special few people who look at towering mountains and think, "I want to climb those." They love the excitement, the uncertainty, and the thrill of the entire experience. They dream of standing on a peak and feeling the wind whip around them as they look out at a view only a few people in the world have ever seen.

These brave people are mountain climbers. They take great pleasure and satisfaction in the same

Climber Beda Fuster takes a moment to absorb the thrill of being at one of the highest peaks in the entire world—a thrill only a few have experienced.

extreme conditions that send most people running back to their slippers and cups of cocoa. Each person who climbs knows that reaching the summit is not only a personal triumph, but a victory for their homelands, as well. This drive to be the first from one's country to reach the top has sometimes created conflict and controversy as people neared K2's summit.

The Earliest Climbers

It is easy to look at a mountain and imagine climbing it. It is much harder to put the idea into action. One of the earliest significant attempts on a major Himalayan peak was made by Albert Mummery in 1895. Mummery and his team attempted to climb Nanga Parbat, but tragically, he and two of his companions disappeared and were presumed dead.

Mummery was one of the first men to attempt climbing the mountain others only imagined ascending.

Aleister Crowley, seen here during his time on K2, was an explorer who always challenged himself and the world around him.

In 1902, British mountaineer Oscar Eckenstein tried to climb K2. He made the trip with new types of crampons and an ice axe he had invented. On his team was Aleister Crowley, an eager explorer who would, years later, turn his attention to black magic.

This expedition ran into problem after problem. Bad weather was followed by snow blindness and illnesses, including malaria and the flu. In more than two months on the mountain, the team had only eight days of good weather before finally giving up and going back down.[1]

Seven years later, an Italian team headed for the summit. The expedition was led by Luigi Amedeo, Duke of Abruzzi. Amedeo's team made it only to 20,500 feet (6,248 meters).

Walter Bonatti almost lost his life on K2, spending the night on the mountain without a tent or supplies to protect himself or his porter.

The next two attempts, made in 1938 and 1939, also failed although they got closer to the summit. Both were made by American teams, and they set new records by hitting 27,500 feet (8,382 meters). The 1939 expedition ended when one of the porters, Pasang Dawa Lama, persuaded leader Fritz Wiessner to turn back only 800 feet (243 meters) from the summit. Lama, a Buddhist, was convinced evil spirits would come out of the dark and kill them.[3]

Success, at Last!
The next expedition saw the loss of Art Gilkey and the heroism of Pete Schoening. The following year, in 1954, an Italian team finally reached K2's summit. For the first time in K2 history, the team brought tanks of oxygen with them, making the ascent more manageable.

Lino Lacedelli and Achille Compagnoni's success was heralded throughout their country, bringing Italy great pride. However, it was not long before a scandal was connected to their victory. For decades, a feud raged on between the two Italians and their teammate Walter Bonatti, and his porter, Amir Mahdi. Accusations were made by Bonatti that Lacedelli and Compagnoni had moved their K2 camp without warning, leaving Bonatti and Mahdi to spend the night on the bitterly cold mountain without a tent or any supplies. Mahdi lost all of his toes and most of his fingers to frostbite. Finally, in 2004—fifty years after the ascent—Lacedelli admitted that Bonatti was right. Lacedelli had deliberately moved the camp in order to reach the summit first.[4]

It was another 23 years before K2 saw visitors again. A Japanese expedition made it to the top in 1977, thanks to supplemental oxygen and a climbing technique referred to as "siege tactics." This method involves hundreds and hundreds of porters establishing camps all the way up the mountain. These camps were stocked with food and bottled oxygen, and were linked by a series of ropes.

In 1978, Americans finally reached the top of K2. Led by Jim Whittaker, the team faced a number of problems, from a series of storms to bickering among team members to hypothermia. Two members of the team, Louis Reichardt and Jim Wickwire, made it to the top. Wickwire made it back to camp but was so weakened by pneumonia and pleurisy that he had to be evacuated by an emergency helicopter.[5]

The 1980s saw four more expeditions to K2. A Japanese team reached the top in 1981 using a new route on the southwest ridge. The following year, another Japanese team reached the top, this time approaching from the much more difficult north side of K2.

Cursed for Women?

K2 is not always kind to women. In fact, some people began to wonder if the mountain was somehow cursed for females.

Women can make excellent mountain climbers. Their bodies often acclimatize to high altitudes faster than men's do; however, they do not always have as much muscle strength as some male climbers. In 1986, three women, along with a group of men, fought their way to K2's summit. These were Wanda Rutkiewicz of Poland, Julie Tullis of Great Britain, and Liliane Barrard of France. Each traveled with teams from their respective countries. During their descent, Barrard and her husband, Maurice, disappeared during during a snowstorm. They were never seen again until their remains

Julie Tullis achieved her dream of reaching K2's summit, but did not survive the trip back.

were discovered years later.

When Tullis reached the top, she turned to her friend, climber Kurt Diemberger, and exclaimed, "Kurt, our dream is finally fulfilled! K2 is now ours!"[6] Their triumph was short-lived. A few minutes later, both climbers were slipping on the ice, barely escaping the earlier fate of the Barrards. Although they made it back to camp, Tullis died two days later.

A Deadly Year

K2 was not just cruel to women in 1986. That year became known as "the worst summer." By the time the climbing season was over, 27 people had set off for the top, but only 14 returned.

The first deaths were two climbers from Oregon, John Smolich and Alan Pennington. As they climbed, a truck-sized piece of rock sheared off a wall, creating an avalanche. Both men were buried. Although a rescue team reached Pennington moments later, it was already too late. Smolich's body was never found.

Maurice and Liliane Barrard died shortly after. Then, sixteen days later, Polish climber Tadeusz Piotrowski slipped and, losing his crampons and ice axe, went over an edge and disappeared. Less than two weeks later, Italian Renato Casarotto was approaching base camp. He had noticed bad weather approaching and turned around, having promised his wife this was his last run. He fell into a deep crevasse. Although a rescue party was launched immediately and he was brought back to the surface, he died moments later from his injuries.[7] Falls, freezing temperatures, and altitude sickness claimed the others' lives during that frightful year.

By August 10, the weather on K2 was unusually violent. On the sixth day of a wicked storm, temperatures dropped to 20 degrees below zero (−28°C) and the wind whipped tents flat to the ground. When the snow finally stopped, the six climbers who had been waiting for a break knew this was it. They were out of food, water, and fuel. Alan Rouse, an Englishman, was too disoriented and exhausted to climb down. The others had no choice but to leave him behind in the tent.

A few minutes into the walk, Austrians Hannes Weiser and Alfred Imitzer grew too tired to fight through the waist-high snow. They simply sat down—and stopped. Dobroslawa Wolf, a Polish woman in the team, disappeared a few minutes later. Only two men survived the descent. Austrian Willi Bauer reached a base camp, and before collapsing, he told them Diemberger was somewhere behind him. Both men were evacuated by emergency helicopter and taken to the hospital. They both had to undergo amputations from severe frostbite to their hands and fingers.[8]

Meet the Porters

Getting thousands of pounds of gear, equipment, and food to base camp is not easy. Most climbers cannot possibly do it on their own, as it would mean multiple trips back and forth carrying heavy loads. To help with the transporting, expeditions hire porters, or "coolies." Large expeditions commonly hire hundreds of them at a time. The porters help with carrying, cooking, and guiding. Some have been known to stay with climbers long enough to help rescue them.

Now and then, porters will stop during the journey and go on strike. They will refuse to go another step unless they get more pay, better equipment, or other demands. Often this means bargaining back and forth until both sides agree on a fee. As of 2024, the average porter in Nepal earns a wage of around $30 a day. [9]

A New Route

After the deadly summer of 1986, climbers were wary of attempting K2 again, but several expeditions still made their way up the mountain. In 1990, a Japanese team established a new route up the northwest face of K2. They were followed a year later by a French team that used the same route, but who made the climb alpine-style, or without the use of fixed ropes or camps.

In 1995, a young mother named Alison Hargreaves became the first woman to

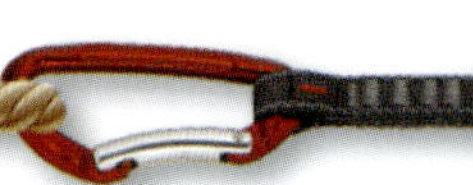

Although Alison Hargreaves was an expert mountain climber, wicked weather on the Savage Mountain claimed her life, as well as a handful of other climbers.

climb Everest, Kangchenjunga, and K2 and reach each peak without using any supplemental oxygen. It was clear and beautiful at K2's summit, but below an unpredicted storm was making its way to the climbers. As Hargreaves and others began their descent, a blinding 140-mile-per-hour wind struck, destroying their tents. Hargreaves, along with five others, never returned.[10]

The 2008 Tragedy

The summer of 2008 brought the world's attention to K2. On August 1, thirty-one climbers from eight different expeditions headed up to reach the summit. Less than thirty hours later, 11 of those climbers were dead.

What happened? American climber Nicholas Rice posted blogs about what happened, giving the world clear reports of who died, as well as when and where. The first fatality occurred when Serbian Dren Mandic fell, followed by a

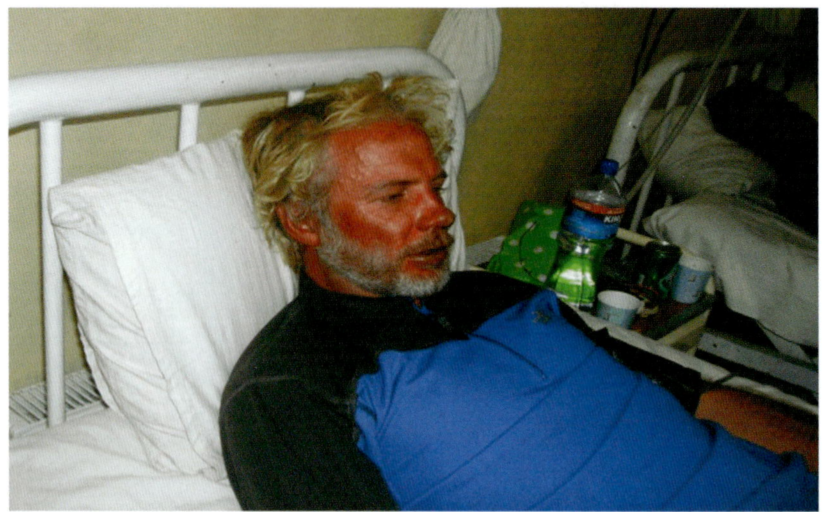

Wilco van Rooijen was one of the only climbers to survive and tell the world what happened on the mountainside.

porter named Jehan Baig who attempted to rescue him.[11] Next, a huge ice ledge crashed down, sweeping away the fixed ropes that showed climbers where to go next. Dutch climber Wilco van Rooijen, who survived the journey, reported, "People were running down, but didn't know where to go, so a lot of people were lost on the mountain on the wrong side, the wrong route, and then you have a big problem."[12] Nine more people were either killed by falling ice, or in an attempt to rescue others. Too soon, night fell, along with the temperature. The climbers who survived the earlier disaster now had to get through a bitterly cold night and then find the closest base camp.[13]

After two such major mountaineering disasters, people began to question whether climbing K2 was a sane, safe mountain to climb—or not. There were easier mountains to conquer. Why risk so much?

In 2011, an international team made up of three men and one woman reached K2's top. They were the first to do so since the 2008 disaster. They climbed up the Chinese side in waist-high snow in temperatures of –25°F (–32°C). Gerlinde Kaltenbrunner from Austria became the first woman to climb all fourteen "eight thousanders"—meaning the fourteen mountains with heights reaching 8,000 meters (26,246 feet) or higher— without using extra oxygen.[14]

The World's Deadliest Mountains

How does K2 compare to the tallest mountains on Earth?[15]

Mountain	Location	Height	Fatality Rate	First date to summit
Everest	between China and Nepal	29,032 feet (8,848meters)	3.8%	1953
K2	between China and Pakistan	28,251 feet (8,611 meters)	29.7%	1954
Kangchenjunga	between Nepal and India	28,169 feet (8,586 meters)	28%	1955
Annapurna	Central Nepal	26,545 feet (8,091 meters)	40%	1950
Nanga Parbat	Kashmir	26,660 feet (8,126 meters)	20.3%	1953

Shrouded in clouds, soaring high into the sky, K2 thrills and frightens climbers throughout the world.

Scaling K2 is clearly dangerous. Obviously, only the most seasoned climbers attempt this journey. It takes a huge combination of thorough research, adequate time, physical training, mental preparation, and proper gear and equipment.

Research

Before attempting to climb a mountain like K2, it is crucial for prospective climbers to thoroughly research the undertaking. This involves reading books, watching documentaries, interviewing other climbers, and consulting with experts. A comprehensive understanding of K2 will enable better decision-making throughout the journey.

Climbers must also consider the time required for both preparation and the expedition itself. Experts typically recommend allocating 65 to 72 days for a K2 expedition. This extensive time frame accounts for the need to hire porters, obtain necessary

Only the most skilled
and knowledgeable
mountain climbers
have a chance of
surviving the trip to
K2's peak and back.

permissions, pay fees, travel to the region, and reach base camp. The remote location of K2 makes the journey both time-consuming and expensive. For instance, flights from the United States to Islamabad, the nearest major airport, can range from $1,800 to $9,000, depending on the season and airline. Once in Islamabad, reaching the mountain can take a week or more, involving travel by bus, jeep, and sometimes even camel, with each leg of the journey requiring separate payments.[2]

On the mountain itself, climbers must carefully plan for the ascent and the summit attempt, accounting for potential delays due to bad weather, illness, or other unforeseen circumstances. It is not uncommon for climbers to spend a week or more waiting out a storm in their tents or allowing time for an injury to heal or a teammate to acclimatize. This flexibility and preparedness are vital for a successful and safe expedition.

Preparing Body

Strength and fitness are crucial for anyone considering the challenge of climbing a mountain, especially the demanding K2. Experts suggest that preparation should involve several months, or even a year or more, of rigorous training to build muscle and endurance. Some believe that proper training for a climb like K2 might require one to two years of preparation. Recommended activities for training include:

- Running
- Cycling
- Hiking
- Weightlifting
- Skiing or snowboarding
- Climbing local rock walls

Participating in climbing classes is also essential. The more mountains one can climb for practice, the better prepared they will be. Experts often advise taking specialized classes in aid climbing, which cover the use of pegs and ropes, as well as ice climbing classes to master the use of ice screws, snow belays, crampons, and ice axes.

Additionally, a thorough medical examination is recommended to ensure that the heart, lungs, and brain are in excellent condition. The high altitudes of mountains like K2 impose significant stress on these organs, and ensuring they are in top shape is critical for handling the demands of the climb.

Preparing Mind

Mountain climbing demands not only physical strength and endurance but also significant mental toughness. History has shown that team members on K2 often suffer from stress, which can manifest as fear, exhaustion, or worry. Such stress may lead to arguments and anger with team leaders, other climbers, or porters, which can have disastrous consequences. Teammates must rely heavily on each other when climbing. Losing calm and focus can result in falls, poor decisions, or rushing without taking proper precautions.

Prospective climbers must assess their emotional resilience before undertaking such challenges. Important self-reflection questions include: Do you panic easily?

Expert climbers and their guides

CHAPTER 4

How do you respond to extreme fatigue and pain? Can you persevere through it? Are you a positive thinker? How do you react when life becomes unusually difficult? Understanding these aspects of yourself is crucial before finding yourself high on a mountain where mistakes are unforgiving.

Getting the Basic Gear and Equipment

While gear and equipment preferences may vary among climbers, the importance of using high-quality gear cannot be overstated. In the harsh conditions of high-altitude climbing, reliable equipment is crucial. The peace of mind provided by sturdy, dependable gear is invaluable, especially when hanging 60 feet (18 meters) down from an icy edge, where a discounted rope would be a source of concern rather than comfort.

The cost of gear for each climber often runs into the thousands of dollars.

Here is a basic equipment list that many climbers consider essential:
- Backpack
- Crampons
- Climbing harness
- Carabiners
- Rope
- Boots
- Ice axe
- Helmet
- Ice screws

Additionally, climbers require clothing and shelter materials, including:
- Hardshell pants and jacket (waterproof/windproof)
- Softshell pants and jacket (for warmth)
- Parka
- Hat
- Gloves (inner and outer)
- Goggles/glasses
- Innerwear clothing (jacket, pants, socks, underwear)
- Water bottles

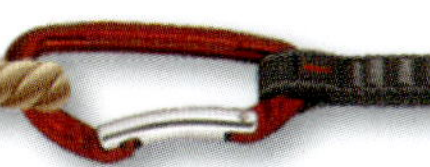

- Tent
- Foam pad
- Sleeping bag
- Headlamp
- Dishes
- Food
- Knife/multi-tool
- Matches/lighter
- Duffel bag
- First aid supplies, medications, sunblock, and lip balm

Permits and Paperwork

Next, climbers have to apply for permission to climb K2. In Pakistan, this is done at the Ministry of Tourism in Islamabad. The fee is usually $12,000 for a group of seven or less. On the Chinese side, applications are made to the Chinese Mountaineering Association in Beijing, which tends to run at least 50 percent more than the Pakistan fees.[6] In addition to these fees, a $15,000 deposit is required for possible helicopter rescue. This money is returned if the helicopter is not needed.

Finally, the porters who carry the thousands of pounds of equipment, gear, and food to the base camp must be paid. Though they only receive a few dollars a day, when there are hundreds of them, it adds up. Extra cash should be brought in case the porters stop in the middle of the hike to base camp and demand more money—it is a common occurrence.

What is the total cost for climbing K2? Conservative estimates place it between $30,000 and $50,000 per person.[7] While some people pay for everything themselves, others may sell photos or video footage when they return. Sometimes businesses will sponsor climbers, who wear clothing with the company's logo, use a particular brand of equipment, or drink or eat a specific product in return for funding.[8]

Choosing a Route

Although climbers have used ten different routes to get up K2, some are used once and then never again. The most common route is the Abruzzi Spur, on the southeast ridge. Three-quarters of climbers choose this path. It is named after Italian climber Prince Luigi Amedeo, the Duke of Abruzzi, who tried to follow this path in 1909. This route is one of the longer ones, covering 2.1 miles (3.4 kilometers) from the bottom to the summit. Along the way, climbers will see areas named the House's Chimney, the Black Pyramid, the Shoulder, and the Bottleneck.

The House's Chimney is a 100-foot-long (30 meters) rock wall. A rope ladder is there to help climbers up the long gash. Some climbers are able to grip both sides all the way up. The Black Pyramid is one of the trickiest parts of the whole route. This pyramid-shaped rock covers 1,200 feet (366 meters) and is made up of rock and ice, with vertical cliffs and piles of snow known for suddenly letting go and creating avalanches.[9]

The Shoulder can be found at 25,225 feet (7,688 meters), and is described as a "hump" covered in ice and snow.[10] Finally, climbers come to the Bottleneck. It is a couloir, or narrow gully filled with snow and ice. It has extremely steep slopes, and ice cliffs arc above the path. Chunks and sheets of ice commonly fall. They have killed climbers and swept away ropes.

After surviving the Bottleneck, the summit is only 300 feet (91 meters) away. This last stretch is tricky though. Gale-force winds threaten to blow climbers right off the route. If they can hang on tight and keep moving, they will be only moments away from the top.

Standing on the Summit

The goal of all K2 climbers is to reach the summit, over 28,000 feet (8,534 meters) in the air. Certainly, it is a view a person would never be able to forget. As the second highest peak in the entire world, the clouds are below you, and you can see the curve of the Earth in the distance.[11] Some climbers bring their country's

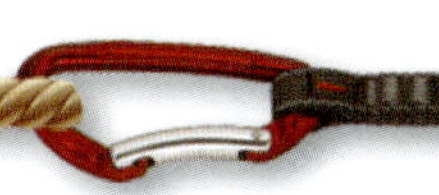

flags, and most have their picture taken standing "on top of the world." Very few spend more than a few minutes on the summit. It is too cold and windy, the air is very thin, and there is a hard climb down to face.

"Keep K2 Clean"

In the summer of 2010, over a dozen men from the Alpine Club of Pakistan, and a number of high-altitude porters, went up K2's Abruzzi Ridge for a new reason—to clean up the trash left behind by previous expeditions. The team spent weeks clearing out rotted rope lines, abandoned tents, leftover trash and equipment, and human waste. The "Keep K2 Clean Expedition" removed over 1,430 pounds (649 kilograms) of trash from the side of the mountain.[12]

Barry Finlay, author of *Kilimanjaro and Beyond,* once wrote, "Every mountaintop is within reach if you just keep climbing." Whether you admire photos of K2 in a book, watch a documentary about the mountain and its climbers, or dream of one day climbing it yourself, there is no doubt it is a magnificent work of nature. Soaring above the clouds, K2 reminds everyone how big and beautiful the world really is.

Why Do People Climb Mountains?

Do you wonder why people choose to climb mountains—or do you understand what drives them? Many studies have been done on people who risk their lives to journey to the top of a mountain like K2, just to come back down again. For some people, it is a desire to test themselves, a personal challenge. How tough or strong are they? What can they cope with—and what is too much? Terribly hard and stressful physical events often give people a chance to learn a lot about themselves. For others, climbing a mountain is a chance to grow and develop. By facing risk and fear, they feel stronger, and more capable. Some just want an amazing adventure. For a few, climbing K2 and other mountains becomes an addiction. The thrill and excitement of being on the edge of danger is like a drug for these people. They only feel "alive" when they are risking their lives.[13]

Many climbers, including Alison Hargreaves, have sacrificed their lives in an attempt to capture the thrill of scaling the astonishing K2.

Facts About K2

Name K2: "K" for Karakoram range; "2" for second peak listed by surveyor in 1852

Other names: Pakistan's name for K2 is Chogori, or "Large Mountain;" China's name is Qogir, or "Great Mountain"

Height: 28,251 feet (8,611 meters), second highest peak in the world

Location: Karakoram range, border between China and Pakistan

First attempt to climb: 1902

First ascent: July 31, 1954, Italian expedition

First American ascent: September 6, 1978, by Louis Reichardt and Jim Wickwire

First female ascent: June 23, 1986, by Polish climber Wanda Rutkiewicz

First death: 1939, American climber Dudley Wolfe

Number of climbers to reach the summit: around 700

Number of K2 deaths as of 2024: 96

Chapter 1

1. Owen Clarke, "Is K2, the 'Savage Mountain,' Becoming Less Savage?" *Climbing*, last modified August 17, 2022, https://www.climbing.com/places/k2-worlds-second-highest-mountain/
2. Grey Satterfield, "Rewind the Climb: Pete Schoening's Miracle Belay on K2," *American Alpine Club*, last modified January 28, 2022, https://americanalpineclub.org/news/2022/1/18/rewind-the-climb-pete-schoenings-miracle-belay-on-k2
3. Greg Child and John Krakauer, "The Dangerous Summer," *Outside Magazine*, March 1987.
4. Charles S. Houston and Robert H. Bates, *K2: The Savage Mountain* (Guilford, CT: Lyons Press, 1954), 187.
5. Ibid., 190.
6. Ibid., 194.
7. Ian Ith, "Mountaineer, 77, saved lives of six climbers on K2 in '53," *Seattle Times*, last modified September 24, 2004, https://archive.seattletimes.com/archive/?date=20040924&slug=schoeningobit24m
8. Houston, 214-215.
9. Ibid., 208.
10. Ian Ith, "Mountaineer, 77, saved lives of six climbers on K2 in '53," Seattle Times, last modified September 24, 2004, https://archive.seattletimes.com/archive/?date=20040924&slug=schoeningobit24m
11. Ibid.
12. Vasiq Eqbal, "Trekking: Honouring the fallen," Dawn, last modified October 30, 2016, https://www.dawn.com/news/1292902
13. Satterfield.
14. Ibid.

Chapter 2

1. Owen Clarke, "Is K2, the 'Savage Mountain,' Becoming Less Savage?" Climbing, last modified August 17, 2022, https://www.climbing.com/places/k2-worlds-second-highest-mountain/
2. "The Karakoram Range," Mountain Professor, accessed May 23, 2024, https://www.mountainprofessor.com/the-karakoram.html
3. Clarke.
4. "People of the Karakoram Range," Britannica, accessed May 23, 2024, https://www.britannica.com/biography/Reinhold-Messner
5. "Askole, Baltistan, Pakistan," summitpost.org, accessed May 23, 2024, https://www.summitpost.org/askole-baltistan-pakistan/707968
6. "Retreat of Glaciers Makes Some Climbs Tougher," *Climate Himalaya*, December 26, 2011.
7. "What Types of Vegetation Are Found on Mt. K2 in the Karakoram Range (India)?" MadSci Network, November 25, 1996.
8. "Snow Leopard," *National Geographic*, accessed May 23, 2024, https://www.nationalgeographic.com/animals/mammals/facts/snow-leopard
9. "Tibetan antelopes," ifaw.org, accessed May 23, 2024, https://www.ifaw.org/animals/tibetan-antelopes#faqs
10. "Plate Tectonics," The Geological Society, accessed May 23, 2024, https://www.geolsoc.org.uk/Plate-Tectonics/Chap3-Plate-Margins/Convergent/Continental-Collision
11. "K2," summitpost.org, accessed May 23, 2024, https://www.summitpost.org/k2/150257
12. "How to Prevent Altitude Sickness: From Acute Mountain Sickness to Severe Altitude Illness," NOLS, last modified April 17, 2024, https://blog.nols.edu/how-to-prevent-altitude-sickness

Chapter 3

1. Owen Clarke, "Aleister Crowley, The Wickedest Climber Ever?" Climbing, last modified May 3, 2022, https://www.climbing.com/people/aleister-crowley-the-wickedest-climber-ever/
2. Owen Clarke, "Is K2, the 'Savage Mountain,' Becoming Less Savage?" *Climbing*, last modified August 17, 2022, https://www.climbing.com/places/k2-worlds-second-highest-mountain/
3. "K2: the mountaineer's mountain," poster, accessed May 23, 2024, https://photographic.co.nz/everestposter/K2%20Poster.pdf
4. Douglas Martin, "Lino Lacedelli Dies at 83; One of First to Scale K2," *The New York Times*, November 28, 2009.
5. James Wickwire, "K2: the American Ascent," *The Himalayan Journal*, accessed May 23, 2024, https://www.himalayanclub.org/hj/36/26/k2-the-american-ascent/
6. Greg Child and Jon Krakauer, "The Dangerous Summer," *Outside Magazine*,
7. Paul Nunn, "Karakoram 1986," *The Alpine Journal*, accessed May 23, 2024, https://www.alpinejournal.org.uk/Contents/Contents_1987_files/AJ%201987%20210-222%20Nunn%20Karakoram.pdf
8. "Trekking Porter Wages in Nepal," *Nepal Everest Himalaya Hiking*, last modified January 10, 2024, https://www.nepaltrekkinginhimalaya.com/pages/trekking-porter-wages-in-nepal
9. Greg Child, "Climbing: The Last Ascent of Alison Hargreaves," *Outside*, last modified February 24, 2022, https://www.outsideonline.com/outdoor-adventure/climbing-last-ascent-alison-hargreaves/
10. Graham Bowley and Andrew Kannapell, "Chaos on the 'Mountain that Invites Death,'" *The New York Times*, August 5, 2008, https://www.nytimes.com/2008/08/06/world/asia/06ktwo.html
11. Ibid.
12. Nicholas Rice, "2008 K2 and Broad Peak Expedition," last modified August 4, 2008, http://www.nickrice.us/index_files/k2dispatch66.htm
13. Kraig Becker, "Climbers Summit K2 for the First Time in Three Years," *Gadling*, August 25, 2011.
14. "The highest mountains in the world," WorldData.info, accessed May 23, 2024, https://www.worlddata.info/highest-mountains.php

Chapter 4

1. "K2 Basecamp Trek," *Alpine Ascents International*, accessed May 23, 2024, https://www.alpineascents.com/treks/k2-basecamp-trek/
2. "Mount Everest," *Alpine Ascents International*, accessed May 23, 2024, https://www.alpineascents.com/climbs/mount-everest/training/
3. "K2 Expedition Required Equipment," *Madisonmountaineering.com*, accessed May 23, 2024, https://madisonmountaineering.com/wp-content/uploads/2020/04/K2-2020-K2-Expedition-gear-list.pdf
4. "Mountain Climbing Gear List," *summitpost.org*, accessed May 23, 2024, https://www.summitpost.org/mountain-climbing-gear-list/226025
5. "China Mountain Climbing Permit," *Sichuan Mountain Guide*, accessed May 23, 2024, https://www.sichuanmountainguide.com/climbing-permit.html
6. "K2 Expedition – Pakistan," SummitClimb, accessed May 23, 2024, https://www.summitclimb.com/climb/k2
7. "How to Get Sponsorship for Mountaineering," *Climbing the Seven Summits*, accessed May 23, 2024, https://climbingthesevensummits.com/how-to-get-sponsorship-for-mountaineering/
8. Stewart Green, "K2: How to Climb the Abruzzi Spur Route," *tripsavvy*, last modified April 9, 2019, https://www.tripsavvy.com/climbing-facts-about-abruzzi-spur-route-755961
9. Ibid.
10. "K2 Clean UP Expedition 2010," *summitpost.org*, accessed May 23, 2024, https://www.summitpost.org/k2-clean-up-expedition-2010/674745
11. Paul Roberts, "Risk," Psychology Today, November 1, 1994.

Books

Bowley, Graham. *No Way Down: Life and Death on K2.* New York: HarperCollins, 2010.

Cohn, Jessica. *Mountain Climbing (Incredibly Insane Sports).* New York: Gareth Stevens, 2013.

Doeden, Matt. *Can you Survive Extreme Mountain Climbing? An Interactive Survival Adventure.* North Mankato, MN: Capstone Press, 2012.

Houston, Charles S., and Robert H. Bates, et al. *K2: The Savage Mountain.* Guilford, CT: Lyons Press, 1954.

Jefferis, David. *Rock Climbing/Mountaineering (Super Sports).* Portsmouth, NH: Heinemann Library, 2002.

Lacedelli, Lino, and Giovanni Cenacchi. *K2: The Price of Conquest.* Seattle: The Mountaineers Books, 2006.

Venables, Stephen. *Voices from the Mountain: 40 True-Life Stories of Unforgettable Adventure, Drama, and Human Endurance.* London: The Reader's Digest Association, 2006.

Viesturs, Ed (with David Roberts). *K2: Life and Death on the World's Most Dangerous Mountain.* New York: Broadway Books, 2009.

Webster, Christine. *K2 (Natural Wonders).* New York: Weigl Publishers, 2008.

Young, Jeff C. *Belaying the Line: Mountain, Rock, and Ice Climbing (Adrenaline Adventure).* Minneapolis: Checkerboard Library, 2011.

Works Consulted

Becker, Kraig. "Climbers Summit K2 for the First Time in Three Years." *Gadling.* August 25, 2011. http://www.gadling.com/2011/08/25/climbers-summit-k2-for-first-time-in-three-years/

Bowley, Graham, and Andrea Kannapell. "Chaos on the 'Mountain that Invites Death'." *The New York Times,* August 5, 2008. http://www.nytimes.com/2008/08/06/world/asia/06ktwo.html?ref=k2

Bradford Washburn American Mountaineering Museum, The Bwamm Blog. December 5, 2007. http://bwamm.blogspot.com/2007/12/famed-schoening-ice-axe.html

Child, Greg, and Jon Krakauer. "The Dangerous Summer." *Outside Magazine,* March 1987. http://web.archive.org/web/20030824070929/http://web.outsideonline.com/news/specialreport/alison/K2omag.html

Child, Greg. "The Last Ascent of Alison Hargreaves." *Outside Magazine,* November 1995. http://rmvl.home.xs4all.nl/en/alison.html

——. "Dateline 1902: First Attempt to Climb K2." About.com Climbing. http://climbing.about.com/od/historyofclimbing/a/Dateline-1902-First-Attempt-To-Climb-K2-Part-I.htm

——. "K2: Second Highest Mountain in the World." About.com Climbing. http://climbing.about.com/od/mountainclimbing/a/K2FastFacts.htm

——. "K2: The Abruzzi Spur Route Description." About.com Climbing. http://climbing.about.com/od/mountainclimbing/ss/K2AbruzziSpur_3.htm

Green, Stewart. "Climbing the 7 Summits." About.com. http://climbing.about.com/od/mountainclimbing/a/7SummitCosts.htm

McLellan, Dennis. "Pete Schoening: 77, Saved Fellow Climbers from Icy Plunge on K2." *Los Angeles Times,* September 26, 2004. http://articles.latimes.com/2004/sep/26/local/me-schoening26

Martin, Douglas. "Lino Lacedelli Dies at 83; One of First to Scale K2." *New York Times,* November 28, 2009. http://www.nytimes.com/2009/11/29/sports/othersports/29lacedelli.html?_r=0

Rice, Nicholas. "2008 K2 and Broad Peak Expedition: Day Sixty-Six: Summit Push—The Final Cost." August 4, 2008. http://www.nickrice.us/index_files/k2dispatch66.htm

Roberts, Paul. "Risk." *Psychology Today.* November 1, 1994. http://www.psychologytoday.com/articles/200910/risk?page=2

On the Internet

Askole Village
   http://www.summitpost.org/askole-village-3048-m-baltistan-pakistan/564135
Christian Stangl on top of K2 summit view July 31, 2012. 1:08 video.
   http://www.youtube.com/watch?v=gzFRvWq1RWQ
Explorers Web: "Permit and Paperwork"
   http://www.k2climb.net/expguide/permit.htm
Explorers Web: "Raising the Funds"
   http://www.mounteverest.net/expguide/raising.htm
Explorers Web: K2 Timeline
   http://www.k2climb.net/expguide/timeline.htm
Gilkey Memorial
   http://www.summitpost.org/gilkey-memorial/537045
K2 Clean-Up Expedition 2010
   http://www.summitpost.org/k2-clean-up-expedition-2010/674745
K2: The Mountaineer's Mountain
   http://photographic.co.nz/everestposter/K2%20Poster.pdf
The Karakoram: K2
   http://www.summitpost.org/k2/150257
Mountain Climbing Gear List
   http://www.summitpost.org/mountain-climbing-gear-list/226025

GLOSSARY

acclimatize—To adapt or become used to a new climate or environment.

alpine-style—To climb without extra equipment or people.

amputation—The process of cutting off a part of the body in order to survive.

avalanche—A large mass of snow or ice that detaches from a mountain slope and suddenly slides or falls.

belay—To secure or lower a person by attaching them to one end of a rope.

capillary—A tiny blood vessel.

climate—The usual weather conditions of an area.

concussion—Injury to the brain or spinal cord due to a blow or fall.

couloir—A narrow gully full of snow and ice.

crampon—A spiked iron plate worn on boots or shoes for aid in climbing or to prevent slipping on ice.

crevasse—A deep crack or fissure, especially in the ice of a glacier.

disoriented—Distracted, unstable, or confused.

edema—Swelling caused by too much fluid in body cells and tissues.

erosion—The wearing away of a surface by water and wind over time.

evacuate—To remove (persons or things) from a place, such as a disaster area, for reasons of safety or protection.

expedition—A journey made for a specific purpose.

frost bite—Injury to any part of the body after excessive exposure to extreme cold.

glacier—A thick layer of ice formed from snow that moves very slowly over ground.

global warming—An increase in the average temperature worldwide.

hypothermia—A serious condition of having the body temperature drop to much lower than normal.

irrigation—To supply land with water by means of man-made canals, especially to promote the growth of food crops.

malaria—A disease of the blood spread by mosquitoes, and characterized by attacks of chills, fever, and sweating.

pleurisy—Inflammation of the lining of the lungs, characterized by a dry cough and pain in the affected side.

pneumonia—Inflammation of the lungs with congestion.

rappel—To move down an incline using a rope secured to the body and to something above.

serac—A pinnacle of ice among crevasses on a glacier, usually on a steep slope.

snow blindness—Temporary dimming of the sight caused by the glare of reflected sunlight on snow.

summit—The highest point or part of a mountain.

tectonic plates—The large masses of rock that make up the surface of the Earth.

thrombophlebitis—A blood clot in a vein.

vertical—Up and down.

ABOUT THE AUTHOR

Tamra Orr is a full-time writer and author living in the Pacific Northwest with her husband, children, dog, and cat. She has a degree from Ball State University and has written over 350 books for young people of all ages. Orr gazes upon several mountains daily, including Mount Hood and Mount St. Helens. Although she finds them quite beautiful, she does not have a great desire to climb them.